THE BEST FRIEND EVER

A Story of Hope, Healing and
Unexpected Friendship in Italy

By Laura Eastman Malcolm

Photography by Donald James Malcolm

This book is dedicated to Susanna.
Thank you for your friendship.

I have been thinking about the true meaning of friendship because of recent extraordinary happenings in my life. Friendship as a cherished value was not an emphasis as I was growing up. I was raised to be competitive, and to believe in a "me first" world, which does not leave much room for friendship as a priority. I enjoyed my friends, and they enjoyed my company, but I was not particularly aware or sensitive to what was really happening in their lives.

Why and how, at my not-so-tender age, did friendship become more important to me? Because I found out what genuine friendship is when someone I didn't know very well reached into my life and showed compassion for me. In a time of great need, she gave of her love and made sacrifices to help me. Let me tell you how my friend Susanna came into my life and how her extraordinary comportment towards me inspired this story. Susanna is Italian, so let us start with my life in Italy, since that is where we met.

For many years I had the marvelous privilege to live with my husband, Donald, in a historic country home nestled in the beautiful hills of Tuscany between Florence and Siena. Built between the 1500-1700's, L'Uccellare was surrounded by bountiful fruit orchards, neatly groomed olive groves and the prestigious manicured vineyards of the Chianti Classico wine region. We chose to purchase this isolated property because we both longed for the freedom to explore our creativity surrounded by such serenity and beauty. Donald had also expressed a desire to have a place and a garden in the countryside. In the twelve years living at L'Uccellare, he worked intensely to transform weed patches into six incredibly perfumed, rose-filled gardens. Roses became an addiction, which means you never get enough of them.

One glorious day in July, Donald invited me to sit down with him on the couch in our living room, looking on to the beautiful fountain garden. He said he wanted to talk to me about something,

L'Uccellare,
built between
1500 and 1700

and he spoke to me in Italian. This always meant, "Listen up and pay attention!" I could tell by the intensity of his tone and the deepened furrows in his brow that it was something important. My favorite cat, Gioia, one of the many abandoned cats we had adopted while living at L'Uccellare, jumped onto the couch to cuddle up between us. In a well thought-out manner, Donald expressed his growing concerns regarding the difficulties associated with our isolated life at L'Uccellare— rough dusty roads (if not muddy), arrogant hunters with their dogs and guns showing no respect for property boundaries, ongoing contention with our neighbors over water rights. I didn't expect to hear this, but I certainly understood what he was talking about.

Finally he said, "I think it is time for us to consider selling our home and moving."

Sitting there stunned, I said, "Oh my, wow, this is news!"

Here was a situation where Donald and I would need to come into agreement—what I call a "prayer point." I told Donald, "I think we need to pray about this. We need wisdom and discernment." Selling L'Uccellare was no small decision and would have many implications on our lives. We both agreed there was no urgency for a quick decision. We bowed our heads, prayerfully put the possibility of selling our home before the Lord, and believed we would come to a wise and harmonious decision.

With the day's responsibilities calling, Donald and I moved on to other activities. But I first climbed the steps to my study in the *colombaia*, the "pigeon's roost" at the very top of the house, to take a few minutes to reflect further on our conversation. *Where would we move to*, I wondered, *and how would Gioia and all our other cats react to such a move?* I looked out over the surrounding Tuscan countryside and the luscious fruit orchards we had inherited with the house. I thought of those out-of-this-world apricots of many varieties...the persimmons...the deep purple, fragrant plums... the sour and sweet cherries, abundant enough for us and the flocks of birds...and the quinces that we made into sauce and chutneys. I would miss all the wonderful things we loved about this place.

Gazing down from my study, I could not deny the logic in Donald's thinking. It is true that living in Tuscany is a marvelous experience. Guests would come to our home and say what a paradise it was, and we agreed. However, we told them, the upkeep of such a paradise was no small challenge. Donald maintained all the artistic gardens he created on his own in his spare time between commitments, and the commute to Florence for work was at least forty-five minutes. Not everything was idyllic.

Considering all of the above and having listened to Donald's heart-felt concerns, I found myself quietly praying and seeking God's peace:

"My peace I give unto you."
– John 14:27

I had to admit that after twelve years living in the Chianti region, we still felt like foreigners. People are very reserved and private, and even after years don't know your name or ever ask how your day is going. I quickly got over the jolt from the idea of selling our home.

I realized that, considering everything, I was not that emotionally attached to our lovely home. Attached emotionally to Donald and our kitties? Yes. I began to feel an interior peace about it, and I realized that Donald was right. A new chapter was about to open up. It was time to move. But where?

The front entrance to L'Uccellare: Laura had her study in the colombaia at the top of the house.

The fountain garden at
L'Uccellare with the
roses in full bloom

W e had always wanted to live by the sea, so we decided to search for a home on the Italian coastline. We put our villa on the market for sale and began making weekend forays to the coastal towns and villages northwest of Florence. We searched and searched and searched, but nothing seemed right.

One day, as we drove on the coastal Autostrada high up overlooking the Mediterranean Riviera, Donald and I were prayerfully and hopefully in the "All right, Lord, surprise us!" mode. We decided to exit and descended the hill on a long curving road into the unknown territory of the seaside town of San Remo. We parked our vehicle in the historic square of Piazza Colombo and walked along the promenade, admiring the dazzling bay and the majestic palm trees lining the streets. We were amazed by the magnificent historic buildings, such as the Art Nouveau Casinò Sanremo, built in 1905 by the French architect Eugène Ferret. As we mingled amongst the townsfolk strolling with an unhurried rhythm, we found ourselves attracted to the friendly, welcoming atmosphere and the luminous beauty of the town. We had heard that the impressionist painter, Claude Monet, had lived on the coast near San Remo for a period of time and painted in his studio there. If this Riviera outpost was good enough for Monet, it would surely be good enough for us. We had discovered a gem of a town and despite the fact that we did not know a single soul in the area, much less a friend, we decided then and there to look for our new home in San Remo.

Suffice it to say that we yo-yoed back and forth between Tuscany and San Remo for a prolonged period of time while we showed our villa to prospective buyers and searched for a home to buy in San Remo. It was all very stressful.

But one day an agent took us to see a one-hundred-year-old Art Nouveau villa. As we rounded a corner and Villa Gioiello suddenly came into view, Donald and I both commented, "That house is beautiful and interesting!"

Perched on a hillside overlooking the sea, *Villa Gioiello* ("The Jewel") was built with the intention of creating a dwelling of restorative calm in harmony with the surrounding landscape. Although the villa needed restoration, its splendid architectural design radiated a beauty that was both inspiring and uplifting. The villa was made of several stories stacked up like a tower, and many rooms offered an unobstructed view of the magnificent gulf of San Remo. With its variety of century-old palms and its small terraced garden, Villa Gioiello seemed to be a mini paradise. On the periphery of the terrace garden stood a classic, wrought iron, Art Nouveau gazebo. There, one could relax and gaze out, day and night, over the monastery below and across the harbor to the horizon with the dancing entertainment of sailboats and fishing boats.

Over the next week we researched the process of buying the villa, considered all the challenges of restoration, and found out that we were in competition with a group of Russians who had a development project proposed for the villa. Donald and I agreed to "relinquish it into God's hands." When we received the news that the Russians had to renounce their development plan for the villa, we went to the real estate agent's office in central San Remo and gave our definitive bid. We were elated! We had just made our big decision to buy a magnificently beautiful home, resonating with light—truly "The Jewel."

Donald suggested we take a walk to reflect on the important step we had just committed to. A little way down the street we passed a jewelry shop, and Donald stopped to admire a ring in the shop's particularly imaginative window display. I looked at the name of the tiny storefront: Vivaldi Concept. We had not previously paid attention to this shop. My husband has very good taste, and the ring that caught his eye was stunning and unusual in its design. We looked at each other. *Should we go inside?* We had just committed to buying Villa Gioiello, "The Jewel," and here we were attracted to a radiant piece of jewelry! We rang the bell and were buzzed into a tiny bijou of a jewelry store. Susanna Vivaldi, the owner, greeted us warmly as did her assistant, Cristina. What a fascinating treasure trove of carefully selected adornments surrounded us. Necklaces and pendants, earrings, bracelets, rings and more, all crafted with unusual precious and semi-precious materials by the most talented and innovative contemporary Italian jewelry designers. Susanna offered us an *espresso café*—which one must not ever refuse in Italy— and invited us to sit down with her at the little round table that filled half of the space in her store.

Villa Gioiello

The view from Villa
Gioiello overlooking
the bay of San Remo

We shared with Susanna and Cristina that we had just made a choice to buy Villa Gioiello and were to become San Remo residents. Susanna exudes an engaging personal warmth, and as she focused in an appreciative and respectfully friendly way on discovering more about us, she asked, "Why San Remo?"

We told her of our search and how the friendliness and beauty of the town had won us over, along with the climate. At this point Susanna clapped her hands and said, "Welcome! Welcome to San Remo!" As the minutes turned into hours, we continued our conversation. Susanna and Cristina were very curious about us: Americans, who spoke fluent Italian and had lived many years in the Florence area. Their question was obvious: "What brought you to Italy, and what do you do?"

Our response was not what one would normally expect. First of all, our main focus and reason for being in Italy was spiritual, not tourism or a cultural experience. We shared with them how Donald had ministered since 1975 to Italian and foreign university students in Florence and Rome, first among mostly atheistic Marxists and "leftover" Fascists, then later to students in a Catholic parish. All of this was "wild and fascinating" since we did not lack for amazing and way-out stories. We told them how we hosted Bible studies and events for the skeptics and the "spiritually hungry." They immediately exclaimed, *"Davvero?!* (Really?!) Would you consider starting one with us? We are sure our husbands and a few other couples we know would love to come."

We said, "When we get settled, we will do this with pleasure."

Definitely, we were an "interesting couple" popping into their lives.

Every once in a while Susanna fielded a call or waved to the townsfolk smiling at her while passing by her store. Both Donald and I had the strong impression that Susanna was a point of light for San Remo. She let us in on her personal life—such a refreshing change for us from the closed and guarded Florentines. She shared about her family and her love for her husband, Gianni, who had been miraculously delivered from life-threatening cancer. She spoke glowingly about her two sons, Gabriele and Filippo. She explained that when her boys became full grown, she decided to fulfill her dream, and she studied to become a gemologist. "And then I opened Vivaldi Concept," she said with a smile.

They say you don't make lasting friendships in the later part of life. Meet Susanna, and that rule changes. Of course, I didn't realize then how important our friendship would become and how much it would change my life and lead me into a deep enquiry on the nature of friendship and love. No, in that moment I was still focused on buying our villa and the challenge of the restoration.

Two days later, the owners of Villa Gioiello accepted our bid. The first thing we did after signing the papers was to return to Vivaldi Concept where my loving husband bought me the ring that we had admired. And that ring, to this day, I wear with delight at every possible opportunity.

The luminous ring from
"Vivaldi Concept,"
a cherished gift from Donald

After buying Villa Gioiello, and waiting for L'Uccellare to sell, we traveled back and forth between Tuscany and Liguria, whilst trying to establish a plan for reconstruction of the villa. Life was very complicated, as we also traveled constantly for work and family to Paris, London, Rome, Budapest and Kabul. When we were in San Remo, we passed Vivaldi Concept often since it was on the main shopping street for pedestrians only. Always a quick "Hi!" with a sweet kiss on both cheeks *a l'italiano*, and if time permitted, an espresso and a short chat. Susanna and her husband, Gianni, introduced us to some of their favorite local restaurants, and even invited us to their home for dinner. We brought them to see Villa Gioiello, and they gave us practical suggestions for the restoration of the villa. Donald and I were appreciative of their friendship, but our time with them was limited and cursory because we were not yet settled into San Remo.

Finally, L'Uccellare sold. We were now under pressure to move to San Remo, but not to live in Villa Gioiello, which required a great deal of restoration work. We needed to rent an apartment in the area. But who would rent an apartment to someone with seven cats? Yes, we had adopted many abandoned kittens and cats in danger of dying that had wandered down our isolated road. Not one rental in San Remo would accept us with our adorable kitties, so we decided (were forced!) to buy a cat-friendly apartment in Villa Nazareth in the town of Ospedaletti on the coast next to San Remo.

After what seemed like endless packing, the movers came to take all our belongings from Tuscany to a storage box near our apartment in Ospedaletti. Donald and I were finally ready to make the big move.

"Want to take a last walk around?" Donald asked. Gazing out from the terrace with its view of the Vineyard Garden and the Sally Holmes roses exploding with a thousand blooms, we

had a singular moment, suspended in time, as we contemplated leaving *la bella Toscana*. Donald and I held hands, bowed our heads, and lifted up one more prayer of thanksgiving, trusting God's sovereignty and loving care as we embarked on our new journey.

We jammed into our car full of suitcases and three cages full of kitties. Baby Calico Skies and Beniamino lamented incessantly the entire three-hour trip.

We arrived at our little apartment at Villa Nazareth in Ospedaletti in the dark, and when we liberated the cats from their cages they scattered in all directions, terrified by the sounds of the sea and totally new surroundings. But by the time we went to bed, they had all returned and wanted inside so as to sleep with us in our bed of *a piazza e mezzo* (for one and a half persons). The question became, how were Donald and I going to adapt? Donald kept saying, "I don't think I can live like this."

The apartment's previous owner had been a manager of Ferrari in Torino, and he had crafted the interior of the apartment's small spaces with beautiful teak furnishings, as if it were the interior of a sailboat. But it was a challenge to cook and eat squeezed into the little galley of a kitchen with its pullout table for two. The small round table in the minuscule living area, which served as our "offices," was piled high with papers and barely had enough room for our computers. Most of our clothes were boxed in a storage unit on a street above our apartment.

Donald had worked hard to save some of his roses, which had been planted in artfully glazed Florentine pots and shipped to Villa Nazareth. Donald positioned them on the small patio of our apartment, thus giving it the feeling of a gracious garden that we and the kitties welcomed as a sheltered retreat. We also brought with us our favorite "cat bench" and cushions, which became a cozy cuddle point on the patio for us and the cats. Though a little shaken, we looked out over the splendid sea through the palm trees, which gave great peace and assurance. We needed it, as the sale of our villa in Tuscany and the buying of Villa Gioiello had exhausted us.

The cat bench at Villa Nazareth, from left to right: Jack the Cat, Baby Calico Skies, Salvatore, and Havana Banana

O nce we'd moved into our apartment in Villa Nazareth with our kitties, I continued to drop into Susanna's jewelry store when I happened to be in San Remo. Whenever I entered Vivaldi Concept she greeted me by exclaiming, *"Gioia!"* ("Oh joy!"). This unique expression is heard in the area of Liguria around San Remo. Each time Susanna greeted me this way, I knew it expressed a genuine depth of joy. It touched me and gave me pause to examine the condition of my own heart when I saw my friend. But, I was focused on the huge challenge of restoring Villa Gioiello. That's where my heart and mind were concentrated.

We had been told that in San Remo it never rains and the weather is always wonderful, to the extent that one could enjoy Christmas dinner outside in short-sleeved shirts. Well, the world economy was changing, and so was the weather, and when we arrived in San Remo it did nothing but rain. The first thing to construct was the garage; the villa's existing entrance and exit gate was very dangerously placed on the curve of the road above which Villa Gioiello was perched. This made it impossible to see traffic coming in either direction. A crew began to excavate the hillside under the garden terrace right in front of the villa, exposing the roots of the lofty palms, and leaving four-story Villa Gioiello towering dangerously over a gaping hole that was filling up with more rain water every day. Daily, Donald and I would gaze nervously at the beautiful palm fronds swaying gracefully high above us, whilst listening to the cacophony of earth moving machines below.

Our architect was rather daunted when she realized that we needed ten different crews to accomplish our goals (often working at the same time). But, she took courage and agreed to direct such a complicated operation, budgeted, and predicted a schedule of about six months.

Our intention and hope was to restore Villa Gioiello to its original majestic and harmonious splendor. However, our lives became more and more tense as unanticipated construction problems developed and we found ourselves mired in the messy work of restoration with a daily work force of up to fifty people. Villa Gioiello looked more like the object of a war zone.

I am reminded of a cartoon I saw in the *New Yorker* magazine during that time. It was of a real estate agent and a couple looking into the door of a house for sale that appeared to be a real mess. The caption of the cartoon was of the real estate agent saying to the couple, "It's a major fixer-upper. How's your marriage?"

I am a person who wakes up and starts the day with this verse in mind:

> *"This is the day the Lord has made;*
> *let us rejoice and be glad in it."*
> – Psalm 118:24

But as the renovations dragged on, I had to recognize that I was neither glad nor rejoicing.

I began to wake up in the morning shaking in my bed. I thought I had Parkinson's disease, which had afflicted my father. I went to the local doctor assigned to us through the Italian social medical system, and asked him to do a test for Parkinson's. But he told me that no test existed. He also said that examining me he knew I did not have Parkinson's, because I was walking and moving in a normal way, without evidence of diminished motor skills. I realized I was suffering from extreme fear due to the expense, difficulties and length of time of restoring Villa Gioiello. This surprised me, because I had not ever considered myself to be a fearful person. If you know me, you would not imagine so, but there I was shaking in my boots. I began to wish the whole Villa Gioiello project would go away.

As a married couple, Donald and I lived and worked together in harmonious friendship, notwithstanding the fact that sometimes we would get tripped up and fall into nasty discussions, caused by self-centered disagreements and aggravated by poor communication. Just ordinary stupidity that we regretted deeply afterwards and would repent of, asking forgiveness from each other and then reconciling. I've always admired and keep in mind the model of the virtuous wife from Proverbs:

"Who can find a virtuous and capable wife?
She is more precious than rubies.
Her husband can trust her, and she will
greatly enrich his life. She brings him good,
not harm, all the days of her life."
– Proverbs 31:10-12

But the renovation of Villa Gioiello was one of our more challenging experiences and, regretfully, there were times when I became contentious, and rather unfriendly toward my dear husband.

One day I woke up at our apartment feeling very scrunched in that minuscule space and I announced to Donald, "You can head east to work on the villa. I am going west to the beach to get away from it all—I cannot handle it anymore!" Off I headed to collapse on a sun bed under an umbrella. While I listened to the gently undulating waves of the Mediterranean, my husband, with true grit, plowed forward with the renovations. This was tough for Donald, but bless his heart, he understood that I was overwhelmed.

44

After a year and a half and many euros spent…liberation! The day to transfer our belongings from Villa Nazareth to Villa Gioiello arrived. We got up early and Donald had his morning cappuccino and cornetto while I sipped a cup of herb tea. (Just a few days earlier, I had decided to give up caffeine and quit drinking coffee. I felt that three cappuccinos in the morning was a bit much, and now that we were about finished with the renovation, surely I could relax.) Beniamino jumped up on the sill outside the kitchen window, peering in with his adorable gaze and hoping to claim a tasty morsel of food. "Hold down the fort, kitties!" I exclaimed as we piled suitcases and boxes into our SUV and headed off down the coastal road toward Villa Gioiello.

Later that day, I noticed I'd broken out with a rash of hives on my breasts. I had never before had any allergic reaction and it seemed odd that these itchy red bumps showed up only on my breasts. I decided it was my body's reaction to withdrawal from caffeine.

The second day of the moving process continued, somewhat bewilderingly. Half our belongings were in Villa Nazareth while Villa Gioiello was littered with boxes to be unpacked in every room on every floor. Restoration on the exterior was still underway and workers were underfoot. At the end of the day, I was back in the cramped bathroom at Villa Nazareth with my husband, jockeying for room, as usual, while we brushed our teeth.

"All right! Now we're really moving," I said. "Don't you love how that little cat house fits perfectly under the terrace stairs?" I leaned closer to the mirror and saw that the hives had now turned into welts. They itched terribly, and I couldn't resist scratching them.

Donald saw them too and with a look of alarm told me, "You need to get some medical attention and have that looked at."

I was trying to make light of it; we were finally moving. I paused…suspended in time. I felt a lump.

"And...there's a lump on my breast." There it was, visible, right below the surface of the skin.

Seeing that small lump protruding on my breast amidst that livid rash immediately silenced my enthusiasm. Donald was right. This was frightening, and I told him, "I'll go to the hospital tomorrow morning to have them look at it."

Donald and I quietly went to bed, exhausted and pensive. I slept fitfully, my thoughts turning to my older sister who had died of breast cancer at a rather young age, and all the sadness and suffering that she and the family went through.

The next morning, while Donald continued with the move, I went off in my little Fiat 500, following the road twisting up the hill to the San Remo hospital. The Radiology Department's examining doctor's opinion was that most likely it was nothing important. But, she decided to do a biopsy (by inserting an instrument resembling a gun and pulling the trigger to extract tissue from the tumor...awful), and gave me a prescription to calm the rash.

It would take time for the report to come back, so I got back into the swing of the move into Villa Gioiello. We gathered up the cats and transported them to their new home. Freak out! They were so nervous, due to the new surroundings and all the workers coming and going around the villa, that they refused to go outside and retreated to our bed again, albeit this time a bigger bed.

I waited a week to hear from the hospital. Finally, the phone rang and the head radiologist, in a rather brusque tone, said, "You need to come immediately to discuss the results."

Donald had already planned that day to make the four-hour drive to Florence for a National Leadership meeting. After he left, I headed back up the road to the hospital. It was strange going up there on my own. I have not ever known an Italian to go to any kind of a doctor's appointment unless accompanied by a family member or a close friend. They are right. I keenly felt my aloneness. Madame Radiologist and the Head Surgeon of Gynecology met with me in a dimly lit office and delivered the harsh news. "Your tumor is malignant, and you will need to have surgery."

I was shocked. I did not know these medical doctors, and I could barely follow the instructions they were giving me in Italian, rife with new vocabulary. There were decisions to make. I listened, dazed. I needed my husband, and he was zooming down the Autostrada a hundred miles away. The surgeon barked that he would consider making space for me in his busy schedule, although the date was July 1st, and summer in Italy means a work slowdown. I was dismissed with the exhortation to commit to surgery as soon as possible. I immediately got on my cell phone to call Donald and he turned around, and headed back to San Remo right way.

There I was, finally accomplishing our long-sought desired goal of moving into beautiful Villa Gioiello after waiting and working so long, and I found myself threatened with cancer. How was I to move forward? How was I to face it, deal with it, make a plan of action, and get rid of it? As I left the hospital, I stopped on the steps. I looked up at the Santuario of San Remo high above; down at the city sprawling below and teeming with life; out to the lighthouse on the point, guarding, protecting; and across the bay where I followed the horizon to see Villa Gioiello on the hill in the distance. I bowed my head and prayed, "God, help me."

I knew I needed to tell my brother, John, and my sister, Louise, that I had breast cancer. When I called my brother, John, he insisted that I come to New York to receive treatment from Sloan Kettering where he had connections with important doctors who had treated my sister, Linda. When my sister, Louise, heard the news, she wanted me to come to Dana-Farber Cancer Institute in Boston, which was her trusted point of reference. These were considered the best hospitals in the world to treat breast cancer. But I wanted to remain in Italy. I did not want to leave my husband in the midst of moving into our newly restored home, nor did I want to go to New York in the sweltering month of July to face who knows what.

I was totally at a loss and without experience in Liguria as to how to find competent medical help for breast cancer. Susanna was one of the few people in San Remo I knew well enough to confide in, so I called her and said I needed to speak to her as soon as possible. "A private matter," I said.

Sitting in Vivaldi Concept later that afternoon, I explained my predicament. At first, Susanna took it for granted that I would return to New York to receive treatment. But I had already made my definitive decision to remain in Italy, and I recounted my experience at the San Remo hospital. Susanna was incredulous and somewhat taken aback, but as soon as it dawned on her that I was serious about dealing with my cancer problem in Italy, her countenance lit up and her demeanor changed. As only the Italians can do, she leaned towards me at that little round table in her boutique cocoon and spoke to me with her face only a few inches from mine. "Laura, *carissima*, you must not consider medical treatment here in San Remo. IST, The National Institute for Cancer Research, in Genova is the best in Liguria. I should know because I have a breast tumor that is benign, and

I have regular check-ups there every six months with their leading radiologist. I will help you."

For the first time since receiving the radiologist's report, I felt hope. Without even a moment's hesitation, Susanna launched into action. She got on her cell phone right then and there and called her radiologist, Dr. Massimo Calabrese, in Genova. Appealing to him to help her friend in distress, she immediately secured an appointment for me for the very next day.

Since our arrival in San Remo, Susanna and her husband, Gianni, had welcomed us, the foreigners, with outstretched arms. But Italy has a historical social protection that keeps everyone outside the family at an arm's distance, and, thus, there had always been a polite and respectful formality between us. Now I was amazed by her compassion towards me, her genuine care that immediately moved into concrete action. For an instant, I recalled that afternoon when I first met Susanna after we'd put in the bid for Villa Gioiello, when we sat right here at the tiny table in Vivaldi Concept. Surely it was a "divine appointment."

"Let me drive you and Donald to meet with Dr. Calabrese. I know how stressful this is," Susanna said as she drew me close to her with a sweeping gesture of tenderheartedness. "Please, this is the least I can do for you."

Thus began a daily pilgrimage of medical visits, all attended or closely followed by Susanna. Out of my extreme difficulty and Susanna's merciful response, our friendship grew and blossomed.

Susanna had recruited her husband, Gianni, to join her to drive me and Donald, and the four of us departed early the next morning for an intense and exhausting all-day trip for my first doctors' appointments. Giving priority to my needs over her own, Susanna left Vivaldi Concept in the hands of her assistant, Cristina, even though we were in mid-summer which is high season for Susanna's business.

The first stop was in a medical facility in Alexandria, a city I had not even heard of, so I could have a high quality MRI exam. Then we continued on to the Cancer Institute in Genova to meet Dr. Calabrese to determine the gravity of my cancer and decide the best course of medical action. Two days later, I was called back, and Susanna accompanied us again to Genova, carrying in hand an appreciative gift for Dr. Calabrese—a good bottle of wine, a very Italian gesture. The tumors were very small and not aggressive, but cancer is cancer, and I would need surgery. Dr. Calabrese suggested I meet his trusted colleague and surgeon, Dr. Giuseppe Canavese.

With Susanna closely following every development, Donald and I returned to the Cancer Institute in Genoa to meet with Dr. Canavese. He made such a positive impression on me in the exceptionally considerate way he treated me and evaluated all the test results during our medical visit. He needed time to make a proposed plan for surgery, though as soon as possible.

Immediately upon returning to San Remo, Susanna was waiting to meet with me at Vivaldi Concept for follow up. "I have been considering all the options in Italy for finding the best surgical help for you," she shared with me, "and I think it would be good for you to also research the European Institute of Oncology in Milano." Even I had heard of this internationally famous Italian center for female medical intervention, founded by famed Dr. Umberto Veronese. Susanna made a concentrated effort to get me an appointment with the director of the hospital, Veronese's son.

We were now in sweltering mid-summer, and Susanna and Gianni continued to make themselves available to help me get the best care so as to be freed of my cancer. All this was happening with a bewildering pace, but I began to feel enormously protected, buoyed up, and carried along on a wave of love.

This time it was Gianni who accompanied Donald and me on the more than two-hour trip to Milan. Veronese's hospital is a very impressive, modern structure that gives the appearance that it is fully equipped, filled with abundant and qualified staff, and organized in a precise manner. It felt like we were back in America, with everything spanking clean and ultra-efficient. Without delay we were ushered into our appointment with the Director of the hospital, and he immediately laid out what he perceived would be a plan of action, including emphasis on post-surgery cosmetic reconstruction, along with an itemized budget.

Gianni, Donald and I were in the car returning to San Remo and evaluating the proposed plan for my surgery at ESMO—we had perplexing questions about the procedures suggested—when Gianni received a call on his cell phone from his cousin doubting the wisdom of doing my surgery at Veronese's cancer center. At the same time I received a call on my cell phone from my friend, Pamela, in America, who gave some wise counsel. Susanna then called to check in with us and find out how I was doing.

In the midst of this flurry of phone calls, something extraordinary happened. Jesus's words from the Gospel of John suddenly came to mind:

"Greater love has no one than this, than to
lay down one's life for his friends."
– John 15:13

I was astonished. I had not ever stopped to focus on Jesus' declaration of the highest form of friendship as he is speaking to his disciples and exhorting them to love one another. I had certainly read that verse before, but now these words took on a living meaning. This standard for friendship filled me with awe. This is what Susanna was doing for me. I was on the receiving end of her sacrificial and loving friendship.

During the two-hour drive returning to San Remo, I continued to hear those edifying words, *"Greater love has no one than this, than to lay down one's life for his friends."* I could see clearly that I was receiving spiritual, psychological, emotional and physical help in my distress, and I was ever so grateful. By the time we arrived in San Remo, I felt deeply at peace. I decided to go ahead and do my breast surgery with Dr. Canavese at the IST cancer institute in Genova.

My next step was to meet again with Dr. Canavese. He wanted to first do a minor, less invasive surgery. If he discovered evidence of a spread of cancer in the area, then I would need to return to submit to a total breast mastectomy.

Before I knew it, there I was in Genova checking into the hospital early in the morning the day of surgery, accompanied by my dear husband. We had a word of prayer, committing everything into the hands of the Lord. Within a short time, the anesthesiologist met with me, and then Dr. Canavese came to visit me before I went down to the operating room. As I was talking with him, I remembered that during our first consultation, I'd noticed a crucifix hanging on the wall behind him. It struck me because this had become uncommon in Italy in the secularized world of modern medicine. Dr. Canavese had an especially kind and considerate way of comporting himself with me and, as he concluded his last questions and remarks, I asked him, "Dr. Canavese, I have friends who are praying for me; are you a believer?"

He nodded his head as if to say yes, and turned to leave the room. But, before he exited, he stopped at the doorway, turned around, and said, "...and I have a prayer group, and we pray for all of my patients." Imagine my delight at this additional provision. The next thing I knew, they were wheeling me to the elevator to descend to the operating room.

Once in the operating room, the anesthesiologist gave me the IV injection. As I was losing consciousness, I was aware of Dr. Canavese surrounded by all of his medical assistants preparing for surgery. They seemed to be such a tight-knit, happy and supportive family. Dr. Canavese was the central figure, giving leadership and taking the responsibility to protect and provide for us all with his experience and loving care.

The next thing I remember, I was in the recovery room coming back to consciousness. It seemed like all the medical staff coming in-and-out were smiling ear to ear.

As soon as I was able to receive communication, Dr. Canavese informed me that they could tell by just looking at the extracted breast tissue, that there was no evidence of surrounding cancer. Although they would do a formal confirmation, Dr. Canavese was confident there would be no need for more radical surgery.

I was taken up to my room to fully recover, and Donald was waiting for me. Within a few hours, the biopsy was completed, and it was confirmed that I did not have an aggressive form of cancer. I would not have to do chemotherapy, but only light radiation as a preventative measure. As soon as I was able, I called Susanna to let her know the good news. Along with Donald, Susanna and Gianni, and cherished prayer partners, I was elated and relieved.

There I was, lying in bed, post-surgery, quietly resting, drifting in and out of sleep. Light flowed in through the window, which also allowed me to gaze out over Genova to the sea. I felt the release from my difficult, yet victorious, ordeal. I waited to feel the pain as a result of my surgery, but it did not come. The gentle nurses explained that Dr. Canavese was such an expert surgeon that often his patients felt minimal or no pain after his surgery. I was receiving grace in so many special and wonderful ways. It had been only three weeks between the time I discovered I had cancer and the time of my being freed of it.

During those days I spent recovering in the hospital, Jesus's words often returned to mind, "Greater love has no one that this, than to lay down one's life for his friends." This verse from the 15th chapter of the Gospel of John was singing within me. From the moment she heard I had cancer, Susanna made it her top priority to help me. I was overwhelmed with gratitude for her friendship. And I had to ask myself if I was capable of giving such friendship. I found myself sorely lacking. As a typical New Yorker, I had been trained that if I had an objective, and there was a closed door in front of me that prevented me from achieving my goal, I was to simply do my best to bash down the barrier.

Now, faced with Jesus's declaration and example of sacrificial friendship as the greatest definition of love, and being on the receiving end thereof, I knew that I needed a personal transformation. I had been given the opportunity to exercise friendship in a new, serious way.

My stay in the hospital was brief and I soon returned home to Donald and our sweet cats. I had plenty of time to ponder the subject of friendship and to consider my own capacity in this respect. Where does one begin? I think the most important friendships are within our own immediate family. I started by looking at my friendship with my dear husband, Donald, who by all means should be (and thankfully is) my closest friend. When I discovered I had breast cancer, we had been in a long process of changing cities, selling, buying and restoring a home—a very, expensive, uncomfortable, irritating, and exhausting process. Then, at the very moment when we achieved the goal of moving into our beautiful home, I discovered I had cancer. Could the cancer and those difficult five years be related? Had I actually brought on my own cancer due to a bad attitude of frustration, impatience, fear? I know my husband had suffered due to my moods and irritability. Now I had the opportunity to ask for Donald's forgiveness and wake up to being a better friend for my husband. Thankfully, Donald responded in the fruit of the Spirit, that being:

"...love, joy, peace, patience, kindness, goodness, faithfulness, gentleness and self-control."
– Galatians 5:22

Since I refer to myself as a Romans 8:28 girl:

"And we know that all things work together for good to those who love God, to those who are called according to His purpose."
– Romans 8:28

I knew that even though had I found myself in difficulty, the opportunities for blessing surely were present. In God's economy—which is very different from our human understanding of economy—even the problem of cancer can also be used for good, especially in our relationships

One of the graceful
gardens at Villa Gioiello

with those around us. My cancer gave Susanna the opportunity to be an instrument of God's love, by extending her helpful friendship to me and, thus, raising the standard for my own life by setting my sights on Jesus.

In the light of the sacrifices Susanna had made for me, the Apostle Paul's writings to the church believers in Philippi took on special meaning:

"Do nothing out of selfish ambition or vain conceit, but, in humility consider others better than yourselves. Each of you should look not only to your own interests, but also to the interests of others."
– Philippians 2:3-4

Surely this attitude of humility helps create successful friendship.

Looking to be a boundless and unshackled friend, I turned to my concordance for further guidance and read one of the most telling descriptions of the love that is necessary for a true friendship:

"Love is patient, love is kind. It does not envy, it does not boast, it is not proud. It is not rude, it is not self-seeking, it is not easily angered, it keeps no record of wrongs. Love does not delight in evil but rejoices with the truth.

It always protects, always trusts, always
hopes, always perseveres. Love never fails."
– 1 Corinthians 13:3-8a

Just as there are various forms of love, (i.e. *phileo*, which is brotherly love; *eros*, which is sexual love; and *agape*, which is God's unconditional love for us), there are many forms of friendship. Some are very superficial and only seem to be motivated by opportunistic self-interest and, thus, the friendship easily falls into disarray. Each one of us knows, if we take a good look at our lives, which are the true friendships to which we are called. My friendship with my spouse, Donald, is my first priority and with my desire to make that friendship an enduring, lifelong friendship, my attitude and sensitivity to his needs and desires have changed considerably. It is my joy to be in harmonious tune with Donald, and this is the beauty of friendship. But, because each individual has intense needs and we all have differing points of view, there is plenty of opportunity for irritation and conflict. I am learning to be more careful so as not to jeopardize this friendship. I am more aware of my husband's needs. I hope and pray for a friendship with Donald that is constant and fruitful.

After my surgery, my friendship with Susanna, obviously, took on a deeper dimension. The restoration of our villa was finally complete and relieved us of much stress. We could now exercise hospitality, which Donald and I believe is one of the greatest expressions of friendship.

Open your door, open your heart.

We remembered Susanna's request when we first met in her tiny shop. "Would you be willing to have one of those Bible studies for us like you did in Tuscany?" The villa, now our home, was a very beautiful and inspiring place to meet, and we knew such a gathering would give us immense pleasure.

We made the invitation to a small group of Susanna and her friends for a once-a-month gathering we called *Bibbia e Forchetta* (The Bible and the Fork). We started the evening with *alta cucina* (delicious and elegant food). After the meal, we climbed the stairs to the Inspiration Room on the third and top floor of the villa. This room got its name due to its stunning wide-angle view overlooking a monastery and palms and the beautiful Mediterranean Sea. What a setting in which to settle down and open up the Bible. For the majority of those present, the Bible was basically a mystery to unveil. There were many unanswered questions regarding life and God. For most, it was like coming out of a fog into an open sky, which was very liberating. It was always a wonderfully warm and enriching time.

Villa Gioiello's inspiring interior with Venetian blown glass chandelier

The view from
Villa Gioiello

I cherished my friendship with Susanna, and eventually she and Gianni became like family.

As the months passed by, I often reflected on the multiple facets of friendship, especially those of a spiritual nature. I realized that true friendship is radical, and not often experienced in this era where friendships come and go. But when friendship has a solid foundation, which is not based on egoism, or me, it can truly flourish and become a precious treasure.

The relationship with God is intended to be just that, a friendship that grows and matures. The foundation is God's unconditional love and grace. God freely extends His love even if we are indifferent or rebellious. It is like a gift offered; to be received or rejected, that is our choice.

When we embrace God's friendship of love and complete forgiveness, we experience a new and transformed life. The quality of our friendships takes on new dimensions, step by step. Where there were fears and resentments, God's Holy Spirit gives us the capacity to experience faithfulness, kindness, gentleness, and patience, because His love flowing through us is gracious, forgiving, and not jealous or envious. I believe that this is a walk of faith, day by day. Some days we stumble, and we are anything but good friends, but God picks us up to move in reconciliation and harmony, which friendship requires. In Italian, the words for friendship and love have the same roots: *amare, amore, amicizia.*

Susanna gave me her compassionate and loving friendship, with generosity overflowing. That is what God has poured out upon my life. All I can say is: *thank you, thank you!*

I pray, dear reader:

> *"...that Christ may dwell in your hearts*
> *through faith; that you, being rooted*
> *and grounded in love, may be able to*
> *comprehend...what is the width and length*
> *and depth and height — to know the love*
> *of Christ which passes knowledge; that you*
> *may be filled with all the fullness of God."*
> – Ephesians 3:17-19

A scarf from Laura's current "Heart to Heart" collection with fringes embroidered with translucent, light-refracting beads

Epilogue

hile in San Remo, another opportunity
to express friendship presented itself
quite unexpectedly. I was asked if I
would use my expertise in beadwork embroidery
to help a group of needy immigrant women from
North Africa. Most of the women did not speak
Italian and lived in poverty and isolation in an area
of San Remo called La Pigna. I immediately said
yes. I knew that I would be putting into practice all
that I was learning about friendship. This would
not be just a didactic exercise, but one of love and
service. By learning simple beading skills, these
women would have a new income-bearing activity
and an opportunity to better their lives.

Set high above the present day town of San Remo, La Pigna is so named for the way the centuries-old buildings curve up a steep hill like the scales of a pinecone. Susanna was quite apprehensive for me to head up to La Pigna because of the high crime rate in the area.

Then came the day when I went up through the ancient, arched city gate into the narrow alleys of La Pigna. My destination was a palace of the 1600s, which the city of San Remo set aside for these special social volunteer activities. Several women from San Remo, who volunteered to teach the Moroccan immigrant community Italian (and also helped their children with their homework after school), greeted me and generously offered to help me with the group.

In our designated work room, decorated with perfectly restored frescoes on the walls and ceiling, I laid out a variety of luminous beads from my collection and showed my "students" how to thread the unique beading needles I use. I had brought scarves with me, and I demonstrated my technique to embroider beaded fringes on the scarves. Then I put all the materials into their hands and gave them the freedom to choose the beads and colors they liked, and we started the training.

At first, the Moroccan women were intimidated and apprehensive, but quickly trust developed. They were fast learners and I could feel their delight as they worked with the faceted, lustrous beads. They laughed as they worked and often helped each other out. With my guidance, and the help of an interpreter, their own creativity came forth, and along with the scarves they also fashioned beautiful, small beaded bags, and more. Since embroidery requires concentrated uninterrupted focus, I also encouraged the ladies to be aware of their internal thought processes, motivating them to pray and intercede for the well-being of their families and more. The project came to be called Perline di Speranza (Pearls of Hope). Susanna and her friends in the San Remo community ladies club supported and helped by organizing fundraising events with sales of the beaded products.

How fulfilling it was for me to have the opportunity to work with these Moroccan women. In extending friendship, I witnessed the joy and satisfaction the beading work brought to their lives. And they, in turn, enriched mine.

In 2014, Donald and I moved to Southern California, where we reside today. We are still good friends with Susanna and Gianni. The Perline di Speranza project came to an end in San Remo, but on arrival in California I was asked once again to share my beadwork embroidery skills with another group of women, this time in India. For more information on Pearls of Hope, and to support the widows and needy women in Chennai, please visit www.pearlsofhope.info.

Laura giving a lesson in beading
technique at the Sangita Charitable
Trust in India. The lives of these
needy and impoverished women are
joyfully transformed as they discover
their innate creativity and learn
valuable skills. They are paid for their
work and become the breadwinners
of their villages and are no longer
subject to extreme abuse.

Laura Eastman Malcolm was born in New York City and blessed with a wonderful family. She graduated from her mother's alma mater, Smith College, where she majored in Art History, focusing on the Italian Florentine Renaissance.

After developing her fashion beadwork accessory business, she married Donald James Malcolm, and joined him in his ministry work in Italy. By that time Laura's fashion project was developing into a charitable effort helping needy women develop skills to better their lives.

Laura has worked with women in locales around the world, including Afghanistan, Italy and New York. She now lives in California with her husband and travels to India where she trains women coming out of extreme poverty and domestic abuse to do beadwork embroidery in the Self Help Group at the Sangita Charitable Trust in Chennai, India.

Acknowledgements

Deep heart-felt thanks to my husband, Donald, for his beautiful photography and help during the writing process. A special thank you to Lisa Fugard, my editor. Lisa, your writing expertise and understanding of story, careful attention to detail, patience, and loving commitment to the highest quality writing has been invaluable. I'd also like to thank Melissa Tenpas for her creativity in wrapping it all up into lovely design that communicates the true intent of *The Best Friend Ever.*

Copyright

Photography » Donald James Malcolm
Editing » Lisa Fugard | lisafugard.com
Cover & Interior Design + Typography
Melissa Tenpas | melissatenpas.com

Scripture references:
Page 10: John 14:27 KJV (King James Version)[1]
Page 41: Psalm 118:24 NIV (New International Version)[2]
Page 42: Proverbs 31:10-12 NLT (New Living Translation)[3]
Page 57: John 15:13 NKJ (New King James Version)[4]
Page 62: Galatians 5:22 NIV
Page 62: Romans 8:28 NKJV
Page 64: Philippians 2:3-4 NIV
Page 64-65: 1 Corinthians 13:4-8a NIV
Page 71: Ephesians 3:17-19 NKJ

[1] Scripture quotations from The Authorized (King James) Version. Rights in the Authorized Version in the United Kingdom are vested in the Crown. Reproduced by permission of the Crown's patentee, Cambridge University Press
[2] Scriptures taken from the Holy Bible, New International Version®, NIV®. Copyright © 1973, 1978, 1984, 2011 by Biblica, Inc.™ Used by permission of Zondervan. All rights reserved worldwide. www.zondervan.com The "NIV" and "New International Version" are trademarks registered in the United States Patent and Trademark Office by Biblica, Inc.™
[3] Scripture quotations marked (NLT) are taken from the Holy Bible, New Living Translation, copyright ©1996, 2004, 2015 by Tyndale House Foundation. Used by permission of Tyndale House Publishers, a Division of Tyndale House Ministries, Carol Stream, Illinois 60188. All rights reserved.
[4] Scripture taken from the New King James Version®. Copyright © 1982 by Thomas Nelson. Used by permission. All rights reserved.

www.ingramcontent.com/pod-product-compliance
Lightning Source LLC
Chambersburg PA
CBHW041955090426
42811CB00013B/1494